ANIMAL OPPOSITES

Sleepy *and* Busy
ANIMALS

Mark Carwardine

Titles in this series

Noisy and Quiet Animals
Daytime and Night-time Animals
Quick and Slow Animals
Big and Small Animals
Warm-Weather and Cold-Weather Animals
Dull and Colourful Animals
Prickly and Soft Animals

First published in 1988 by

Wayland (Publishers) Ltd.
61 Western Road, Hove
East Sussex BN3 1JD
England

© Copyright 1988 Ilex Publishers Limited

British Library Cataloguing in Publication Data

Carwardine, Mark
Sleepy and Busy animals.—
(Animal opposites)
1. Animals—Juvenile literature
I. Title   II. Series
591   QL49

ISBN 1–85210–624–4

Created and produced by
Ilex Publishers Ltd
29–31 George Street
Oxford OX1 2AJ

Illustrations by Martin Camm, Dick Twinney
and John Francis
Courtesy of Bernard Thornton Artists

Typesetting by Optima Typographic, London
Printed in Spain by Gráficas Estella, S.A.

Cover illustration by Jim Channell
a bear and a raccoon

Contents

Some words in this book are printed in **bold**; you can find out what they mean in the glossary on page 24.

The mouse lemur is a sleepy animal.

It spends several months of the year resting or **hibernating** in a hollow tree.
This mouse lemur is fast asleep.

The mouse lemur is one of the smallest of all monkeys and apes. It lives in the jungles of Madagascar and spends most of its time in the trees.

The raccoon is a busy animal.

It is always getting into trouble.
These cheeky raccoons are looking for scraps
inside an overturned dustbin.

Raccoons like to live near people and will
make their homes almost anywhere. Active
mostly at night, they spend the daytime
sleeping in a hollow tree, or in an attic or
garden shed.

The dormouse is a sleepy animal.

It curls up into a tiny ball of fur and spends
all winter fast asleep.
This dormouse has built a nest in the middle
of some leaves.

Dormice sleep for as long as seven months
each winter. But first they stuff themselves with
food in the autumn, until they are so fat that
they have nearly doubled in weight.

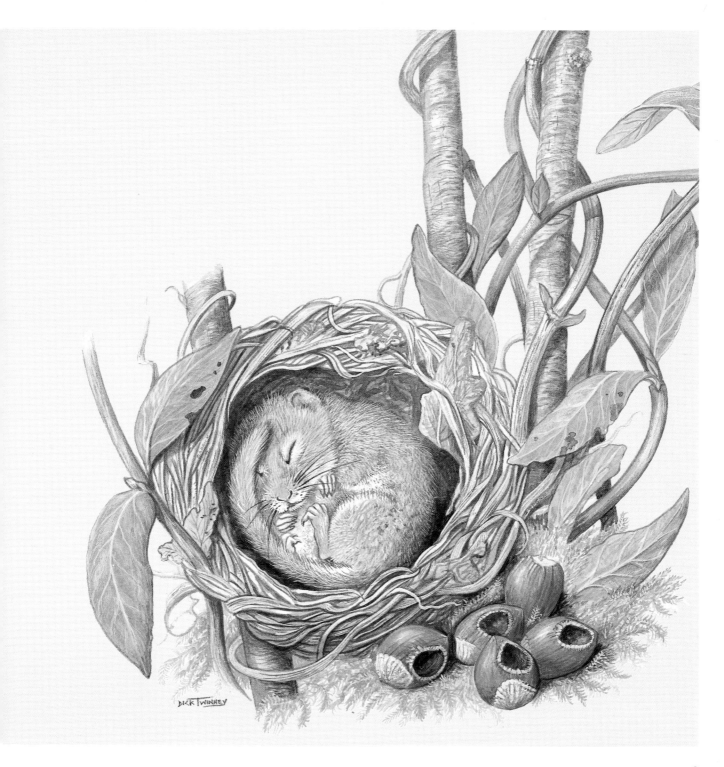

The macaque is a busy animal.

It is a kind of monkey that lives high up in the cold mountains of Japan.
This macaque is carrying some sweet potatoes in its arms.

Japanese macaques are like people in many ways. They learn very quickly and are able to teach one another different tricks. They are even able to walk upright on two legs.

The koala is a sleepy animal.

It spends as much as twenty hours every day dozing or sleeping.
This koala is fast asleep in the fork of a tree high above the ground.

Koalas look just like bears. But they are actually related to kangaroos, and **female** koalas even have pouches on their bellies. They live in gum trees in south-eastern Australia.

The water shrew is a busy animal.

It always seems to be in a hurry and rarely finds the time to sleep or rest.
This water shrew is swimming to the bottom of a pond.

Always busy and on the move, water shrews are active at night and during the day, snatching just a little sleep whenever they get the chance. Their **prey** includes insects, fish and frogs.

The bear is a sleepy animal.

It sleeps during the winter in a cave or under a dead tree.
This black bear is surrounded by angry bees because it has eaten their honey.

Black bears sometimes wake up during their winter sleep and may wander outside during periods of warm weather. As well as honey, they like to eat fruits, berries, nuts, insects and a variety of other plants and animals.

The orang-utan is a busy animal.

It spends much of its time swinging from branch to branch high up in the trees. This orang-utan and her baby are collecting figs.

Orang-utans' arms are very strong and are so long that when the animals stand upright their fingers almost touch the ground. Orang-utans always rise early in the morning and spend the rest of the day searching for food.

The hamster is a sleepy animal.

It goes to sleep in the autumn and does not wake up again until the following spring. This hamster is using its cheeks like shopping baskets, to carry food back to its burrow.

Golden hamsters are common animals in the wild. Found in many parts of Europe and Asia, they live along riverbanks, in fields, in deserts and on mountain slopes.

Dick Twinney

The pine marten is a busy animal.

It looks more like a giant squirrel as it races around in the trees.
This pine marten has caught a squirrel and is about to eat it for supper.

The pine marten belongs to a family of animals known as the mustelids, which includes otters, badgers and ferrets. Found in many parts of Europe and as far east as Asia, it is about the size of a large cat.

Index

Glossary

Female An animal that is, or can be, a mother.
A woman is a female human being.
Hibernating Sleeping through the winter.
Prey An animal or animals hunted by others for food.